£4.50 UK only

Contents

Meet the Animals

There were once a lot of animals in Farthing Wood, all living together as nature intended them to live. Some were the natural enemies of others, but on the whole Farthing Wood was a place of beauty and peace.

Until one day, some men moved in with their tractors and excavators...

"What are they doing to our wood?" said the animals. "They will destroy it!"

But there was no stopping the workmen. Trees were cut down, bushes were flattened – and then Farthing Wood Pond was filled in.

"What are we going to do?" the animals asked each other. "We can't survive without water."

It was then that Fox made a suggestion.

"We must call a Farthing Wood Assembly," he told Badger.

"But we haven't had an Assembly in years, Fox," said Badger. "We only call them when there's an emergency."

"And what's this if it isn't an emergency?" Fox wanted to know.

And, of course, he was right. Weasel, Hedgehog and Mole agreed with him. "We can't just sit around here doing nothing," they said.

So an Assembly was arranged.

All the animals came to Badger's underground home, even Owl, Pheasant and Kestrel who didn't really like being underground. Some of the smaller animals were very fearful, especially when they heard that Adder would be there. But Badger assured them they would be safe, and so everyone came to the meeting.

But it was one of the smallest creatures who provided them with the answer to their problems...

"I know where we could go," said Toad. "There's a wonderful place I know, called White Deer Park..."

"White Deer Park?" said Mole.

"Never heard of it!" hooted Owl.

"It's a Nature Reserve," explained Toad. "It's made especially for animals like us."

"Do you know how to get there, Toad?" asked Fox.

"Oh, yes," said Toad. "I can take you there."

"Then you shall be our guide, Toad," said Badger. "And Fox shall be our leader."

"Just a minute," said Hare. "Are you suggesting we all travel to this White Deer Park place...*together*?" He was looking nervously at Fox and Owl, both of whom Hare considered to be his natural enemies. "What about that snake?"

"Did sssomeone mention me?" hissed Adder.

"She's already eaten half the fieldmice in the wood!" said Hare.

"Then we will each take the Oath of Mutual Protection," said Badger. "That way we shall all be safe from one another."

"Oath of Mutual Protection?" said Hare. "What's that when it's at home?"

"It's a promise," said Badger, "not to frighten or to bully or to...er..."

"Eat one another?" said Adder. She looked disappointed.

"Exactly," said Badger.

So each of the creatures took the solemn Oath of Mutual Protection, which would last for as long as it took them to reach White Deer Park.

"We will all meet at the Great Beech at midnight," said Fox. "Don't be late!"

And so began the journey from Farthing Wood to White Deer Park. It was to be a long journey, full of adventures – some of them funny, others dangerous.

Fox and the Burglar

It was always safer for the animals to travel at night, so all day they had been resting in the quiet part of a small factory. The factory was on an industrial estate, just outside a town. The previous night's journey had been particularly tiring and by the time they had found a suitable place to rest, all the animals were very sleepy.

But it had been important not to be discovered by the work people in the other parts of the building, so three of the creatures had taken it in turns to keep watch whilst their fellow travellers slept.

First, Badger had been on guard, then Kestrel, and finally it had been Fox's turn. But now the work people had gone home and Fox was getting restless. He was tired of listening to Badger's snoring. None of the other creatures were awake yet, not even Owl, although it was already getting dark outside.

Fox decided to look around the rest of the building now that it was empty. After all, the others would be safe enough and he was curious to see what was made here, or if there was any food to be had. Sometimes, there were canteens in places like this where the work people had their meals.

Fox set off into the dark factory, trotting between machines and benches. He found someone's half-eaten sandwich and a piece of biscuit, but no other food.

All at once, he heard footsteps coming slowly along one of the aisles. He guessed it was a man left to guard the building. Fox was careful to keep out of sight.

He wondered what sort of night it was outside. Were they going to have a dry journey? Looking out of a window, he saw a cloud passing across the face of the full moon.

There were some big black doors up ahead, almost certainly leading to the outside. Fox decided to check on the weather and he padded quietly towards them. He pushed one door open with his paw – *and suddenly there was a dreadful howling noise that filled the whole factory!*

"Oh, no!" muttered Fox. "What have I done?"

The noise had woken the other animals and they began to scurry around their corner of the building, trying to see what was happening.

"What's that terrible row?" cried Badger.

"It...it sounds like a g-g-ghost!" wailed Mole, diving under a pile of cardboard boxes.

"Don't be ssstupid," hissed Adder. "You don't get ghostsss in factoriesss."

"A howling monster?" screamed Weasel, scuttling across the floor then jumping on to a shelf.

"It's a burglar alarm!" said Owl. She flew round in a circle. "Somebody must have broken into the building!"

"Oh, no!" said Badger. "We'd better be getting out of here. Where is Fox?"

Everyone looked around but their furry companion was nowhere to be seen.

"P-perhaps the burglar has got him," said Mole.

"More like Fox is chasing the burglar," smiled Owl. "I'll take a look around and see if I can spot him."

"Don't be long," Badger warned her.

"There are men who guard factories and they will be coming to see what's happening. The rest of us had better find places to hide."

The security guard had heard the alarm go off and had been going to investigate when, suddenly, he heard other noises. Sounds of feet scampering to and fro at the back of the building, in the Stores. Then a fluttering noise above his head in the darkness.

"Sounds like a whole gang of burglars have broken in!" he thought, and he immediately ran to phone the police for help.

Fox began to run back to the part of the building where his friends were hiding. Which way had he come? All the aisles looked alike. Was it this one?

Within minutes, Fox was hopelessly lost.

He wandered round and round in circles until, five minutes later, he looked up and saw Owl.

"This way, Fox!" hooted Owl.

Fox was very relieved to see her friendly face again. But he could hear another noise now. It was the siren of a police car as it sped through the streets towards the factory.

"Whatever have I started?" Fox said to himself. "All I did was to open a door."

Owl was perched on a shelf above him. "You set off the burglar alarm by opening that door," she said.

"Did I?" said Fox. "Then shouldn't we be getting out of here?"

"Better to wait until the fuss has died down," said Owl. "Go and hide behind those boxes with the others."

Just then, all the lights in the factory went on. There was the sound of running feet as the policemen and the security guard began to search the building.

"Who's there?" called one voice.

"We know somebody's in here!" said another.

The animals became nervous.

"We ought to get out before they find us," whispered Badger. "We don't want to be caught like rats in a trap."

The others winced at the thought of traps – every woodland animal's nightmare.

"You're right," said Fox. "Come on, I know the way out now."

He led them towards the door that he had pushed open.

They kept their heads down behind the machines and benches but, just as the big black doors came in sight, Weasel said, "Where's Mole?"

Everyone looked around for the little grey creature.

"I thought he was on my back," said Badger. "He must have slipped off..."

"Here he comes!" said Kestrel.

And they saw Mole puffing and blowing as he tried to catch up with them.

Unfortunately, someone else saw him, too.

"*Over there!*" came a shout.

"Oh, no!" cried Kestrel. "Now one of the men has seen him!"

"Let'ssss get out of here!" hissed Adder, and she slithered on towards the doors.

"What about Mole?" whimpered Hare. "We can't leave him behind."

"I'll go back for him," said Fox. "The rest of you get out of those doors."

Fox ran back for Mole, but straight away he was spotted by two policemen and the security guard.

"A fox!" shouted one policeman.

"And a mole!" exclaimed the other. "Crumbs, Fred! What are you running here, a *menagerie*?"

Mole quickly jumped on to Fox's back and the two of them made for the open doors. The others were safely outside, hiding in the shadows of the nearby buildings.

The two policemen and the security guard chased after Fox, but Fox was much too quick for them. Once outside, all the men could see was the animal's bushy tail disappearing into the darkness.

"We've lost him, Dave," said one policeman.

"Wonder how he got in?" said the other. "What do you think, Fred?"

But the security guard was looking across at the next factory. "I thought I saw a light in that window," he said, pointing. "There! Did you see it? Looks like a torchlight."

"So who's creeping around in there?" said one of the policemen.

"I think we'd better take a look," said the other.

Just at that moment, the shadowy shape of a man climbed out of the window.

The animals watched from their hiding places as the policemen ran towards him. He had a bag over his shoulder.

There was a yell of "Got you!" as one policeman grabbed him.

"They've caught a *real* burglar!" hooted Owl.

"So they didn't have a wasted journey after all," chuckled Badger.

"Thanks to me!" said Fox, laughing.

ANIMAL FACTS

The Fox

Foxes can be found in both town and country, usually at night. They will eat almost anything and are natural scavengers. If your dustbin has been overturned in the night, and there are bones or old food wrappings lying around it, the chances are you've had a foxy visitor!

A fox's home is called an earth and it is often found under the roots of large trees in the country. The female fox is called a vixen. The most common variety of fox is the Red Fox, but there are others. One is the Grey Fox, which is found in North America. Another, the Arctic Fox, has a white coat, which is perfect camouflage in the snow-covered land where it lives.

Toad in Trouble

"Hurry up," said Toad, hopping along the country road. "It's almost daylight and time to find a place to rest." But the others were too tired to hurry.

Toad always seemed to have more energy than the other animals. He hopped on ahead happily. But there was danger just around the corner...

Suddenly, Toad found himself falling between two thick metal bars – down, down into a deep, dark pit! "Help!" he yelled, and landed with a THUD!

The others came round the corner nervously when they heard Toad's cry. "Toad? Toad? Where are you?" said Badger. Toad had disappeared!

Then they saw what had happened to him. "He's fallen down one of those things the humans put on roads to stop cattle straying," wailed Mole.

"It's called a *cattle grid,*" Owl informed them. "Very dangerous things for small animals, I've always thought. And it looks like I was right, doesn't it?"

"What are we going to do?" asked Hare. "We can't leave poor Toad down there." "No, you can't!" squeaked a tiny voice from the darkness below.

Toad was peering up at his friends above. "I sssuppose I mussst help," hissed Adder. "He'sss the one who knowsss the way to the Nature Ressserve."

Adder hung down from a rung in the grid and Toad desperately tried to grab her. But it was no good. Adder just wasn't long enough. "Sssorry," she said.

Next, Fox pushed his bushy tail down through the cattle grid, but that wasn't long enough either. "Oh, dear! What else can we try now?" said Weasel.

Owl was busy looking around. All of a sudden, she spotted something and swooped down for a closer look. "Over here!"she called to the other animals.

"This old fence is ready to fall down," said Owl. "Let's give it a hand." "How will that help Toad?" Fox wanted to know. "You'll see," said Owl, smiling.

All the animals pushed against the fence until, with a big creak and a great CRASH! the whole thing fell down. "Now what?" gasped Hare.

"Push it over to the cattle grid," said Owl. So they pushed and pulled the rotten fence to the grid. "Tip it up and slide it through," said Owl.

Toad hopped up on to the piece of fence and out through the grid. "Clever Owl!" he said. "There should always be a slope inside cattle grids," said Badger.

"Then," he said, "if a small creature should accidentally fall in, it will easily be able to get out again." And he was right, of course.

Which Animal?

Clues:

1. This is the oldest of the animals travelling to White Deer Park. He usually lives in a sett.

2. This is the leader of the animals travelling to the Nature Reserve. He's sometimes chased by huntsmen.

3. Thisss creature ssslithersssss and ssslidesss acrosss the ground! But she sounds as if she can do sums!

4. This little creature is showing the rest of the animals the way to the Nature Reserve. He'll hop his way there!

5. This little animal doesn't see very well, and he lives underground.

6. This prickly creature rolls up into a ball whenever there is trouble around!

1 BADGER
2 FOX
3 ADDER
4 TOAD
5 MOLE
6 HEDGEHOG

It was early morning and not yet light. Fox was walking along a country lane, behind the others. Sometimes he liked to make sure there were no stragglers!

Suddenly, a car came speeding around the corner, its headlights throwing a beam across the lane. Fox was dazzled and couldn't see.

The car whizzed past Fox, missing him by inches. "Phew!" said Fox. "That was close! That driver didn't see me in the dark. Look out, everyone!"

The other animals had to jump out of the way of the car, too. Badger jumped into a hedge whilst Hare and Weasel leapt into a muddy ditch!

"That's the trouble with these narrow lanes in the dark," said Badger, climbing out of the hedge. "Drivers don't see us until the last minute."

Later on, the animals were coming into a town. A young boy went past on his bicycle, ready to begin his early morning paper round.

"What's he wearing on his arms?" said Mole. "They're special safety armbands that show up in the dark," said Owl. "They help him to be seen."

"How clever!" said Mole. Fox agreed. "They should make those things for us animals to wear on dark, wintery mornings!" he said. They all chuckled.

Cover the Animals

A game for two players. You need a dice and twelve squares of card or paper (playing cards will do) to cover the pictures on these pages. Each player has six squares of paper (or playing cards) and one page of pictures.

1

2

3

4

5

6

At each throw of the dice, the player covers the picture which has the same number as that shown on the dice. If the square is already covered, the player misses a turn. The first player to cover all the pictures on his or her page is the winner.

1

2

3

4

5

6

In the Picture

Weasel was the first of the animals to see the man. "What's he doing?" she wondered, watching him from behind a tree.

The man took a camera from the case hanging over his shoulder and began to take pictures of a little copse.

"He's a *photographer*!" thought Weasel. "He looks very professional. Perhaps he's taking photographs for the newspapers or a magazine. Yes, that's it! He probably works for one of those magazines that have pictures of the countryside in them."

Weasel watched the man clicking away with his camera. But he seemed to be looking for something.

"He wants some wildlife pictures and he's looking for an animal to photograph," said Weasel to herself. "Hmmm, well I wouldn't mind a nice colour picture of myself in a magazine." And she straightened her whiskers and brushed some earth off the end of her nose, then she stepped out from behind the tree.

At first, the man didn't see her. He was busy photographing a pretty yellow flower. Weasel coughed discreetly, so that the man would hear. He turned round.

"Ah!" he said, and took three quick pictures of her. "Lovely!"

Weasel hurried away, delighted to think that she might be appearing on the cover of next month's *Nature News*, or whatever magazine the man worked for. She couldn't wait to tell the others.

"A photographer?" said Badger. "How interesting."

"I'm sure he'd like a picture of me," said Kestrel. "Everybody does. You see pictures of kestrels in all the best bird books and magazines."

"And owls," said Owl. "He'd definitely want a picture of me, too."

"I expect he'd like one of all of us," said Fox.

"Do you think so?" asked Mole. "Ooh, how exciting! I've always wanted my picture in a magazine."

"Well, now's our chance," said Hare, and he bounced off in the direction of the copse.

The others followed after him. Kestrel flew on ahead and was the first to arrive on the scene. She hovered overhead for a few moments, then swooped down in front of the photographer.

"A kestrel!" said the man, excitedly. And he clicked away with his camera.

A few minutes later, the man was surprised to see an owl fluttering past him. "What a strange time of day to see you, my feathered friend!" he laughed, quickly taking a picture.

Fox was convinced he was the best looking animal and would make a splendid cover picture for a book on wildlife. He spruced himself up and trotted into the copse. There was the photographer, looking up at the sky, hoping to see yet another bird.

"Look this way," Fox wanted to say. "I'm *much* more attractive than some silly old bird." But the man didn't seem to see him.

Fox wanted to attract the man's attention, so he made as much noise as possible as he walked through some dried-up old leaves and twigs. But still the photographer didn't notice him.

It was while Fox was looking back over his shoulder to see if the man had heard him that he walked into the muddy bog. SQUELCH! SQUELCH! And there he was, up to his tummy in slimy mud!

"Yuk!" muttered Fox, pulling himself out. Now his nice red coat was a dirty brown colour.

It was at this moment that the photographer turned and saw Fox. In an instant, he was clicking away with his camera.

"Oh, no!" grumbled Fox. "What a horrible picture I'll make, all covered in mud!"

"Karrk! Karrk!" squawked Pheasant.

"Never mind that old Fox. Look at me!" And he flew extra-low so that he would be noticed. Unfortunately, Pheasant was so busy looking at the photographer that he didn't watch where he was going. Suddenly, he crashed into a tree branch and plummeted to the ground in a flutter of feathers. "Ouch!" he cried.

An astonished photographer took a picture of Pheasant as the bird picked himself up and limped away into the trees.

"What unusual pictures I'm getting today," said the man.

Luckily, Badger, Hare, Toad and several of the others all managed to get their pictures taken without any mishaps.

"That's what comes of showing off," Badger told Pheasant when the bird explained about his accident with the tree. "Now, it's time we were moving on again."

"But I haven't had *my* picture taken yet!" said Mole. "Every time I get into a place where the man can see me, one of you lot comes zooming down from the sky, or jumping out from behind a tree. It's not fair!"

"Oh, all right," sighed Fox. "We'll all keep out of the way and let you go and get your picture taken."

So off went Mole, into the depths of the copse. He hurried in amongst the trees. Now, where was the man? Ah, over there by that silver birch tree.

"Oh, no!" thought Mole. "He's packing up his things, ready to go home. If I don't hurry up and let him see me, I'll be too late!"

Mole scurried through the undergrowth. He could barely see where he was going, but he knew he had to be quick.

Unfortunately, the man didn't see Mole – until he tripped over the little animal!

"Ouch!" cried Mole as he was bumped by the man's boot.

"Aaagh!" cried the man as he fell over.

The photographer tried to save his camera, but he wasn't fast enough. It crashed to the ground and the back sprang open. Out burst the film!

"Oh, no!" groaned the man. "Now the film has been exposed to the light. All my lovely pictures are ruined!" He looked around. "Whatever did I trip over?"

But Mole was gone. Already he was scampering back towards the others.

"Er...I don't think I'll mention what happened with the man's camera," Mole thought.

Which was probably the best idea he'd had all day.

Flying Hedgehog!

Hedgehog's feet were aching. He saw Kestrel flying above him. "I wish I could fly, like you," he sighed. "It would be so much quicker than walking."

Kestrel did a very spectacular dive, followed by a loop-the-loop. She was showing off. "I've never heard of a flying hedgehog!" she laughed.

"It's not fair!" sulked Hedgehog, rolling himself into a ball. "You'd make a good football if you weren't so prickly!" laughed Kestrel.

"He looksss more like a pin cussshion to me," hissed Adder. And everyone laughed. "Shut up, Kestrel! Shut up, Adder!" shouted Hedgehog, grumpily.

Hedgehog was really fed up with being teased. Later on, when it was time to rest, he decided to go off by himself and find a place on his own.

"This looks like a comfortable spot," thought Hedgehog. "How strange that someone should leave a lovely big basket like this lying around."

Hedgehog settled down and had a very pleasant sleep. But his dreams were all airborne...he dreamed he could fly, high up in the sky, just like Kestrel!

After having such exciting dreams, Hedgehog was sorry to wake up. But when he looked around, he found he really *was* flying – in a *hot air balloon*!

There was a crack in the side of the basket and Hedgehog peeped through it. "We're flying high over the fields!" he cried to himself. "Oh, no!"

Hedgehog looked around but, luckily, the balloonists hadn't noticed him. They were too busy enjoying the view. "Oh, what can I do?" he thought.

He wanted to shout "Help!" but was afraid of what the balloonists might do if they saw him. Where were the other animals? How far away was he?

Meanwhile, Badger, Fox and the others were wondering what had happened to their prickly friend. "It's your fault for teasing him, Kestrel," said Hare.

"Adder teased him, too," said Kestrel, sulkily. But she was worried about Hedgehog. "He'll turn up sssooner or later," hissed Adder. "Ssstop fusssing!"

Kestrel flew up into the sky to take her morning exercise. Just then, she saw the hot air balloon floating past. "How interesting," she said, flying nearer.

Suddenly, she saw Hedgehog's anxious little face looking up at her. "What are you doing there?" asked Kestrel. And she flew down to rescue her friend.

"I'll be happy to leave the flying to you in future," Hedgehog told Kestrel. "I think I prefer to keep my feet on the ground!" he laughed.

ANIMAL FACTS

The Hedgehog

Hedgehogs are seen in both the town and the countryside. They are often called the 'Gardener's Friend' because they eats slugs and other insects which threaten to spoil flowers and vegetables. The young hedgehogs follow their mother around in the hunt for tasty worms, slugs, beetles and caterpillars. Hedgehogs sleep rolled up in a 'blanket' of leaves in the winter. At other times, if they think there is danger about, they will roll themselves into a tight prickly ball.

Have you seen this Bird?

On these two pages are various birds that you are likely to see in the British Isles. There is a space beneath each picture so that you can keep a record of the date and place you saw each bird. Happy bird spotting!

Collared Dove

Usually lives close to human habitation. Notice the narrow black half-collar. Makes a noisy 'coo-coooo-coo' sound.

Date....................

Place...................

Woodpigeon

Found mostly in the countryside where there are lots of trees. Has a white patch on its neck. Makes a 'coo-coo-coo' sound.

Date....................

Place...................

Date....................

Place...................

Blackbird

A very well known bird. Has a 'screaming chatter' sound when alarmed. The female is browner in colour.

Date..................

Place.................

Magpie

A black-and-white bird which usually lives in the countryside but which is becoming a more common sight now in town gardens.

Blue Tit

Nests in woodlands, gardens and hedgerows. Has a bright blue 'cap' on its head and yellow underparts.

Date....................

Place...................

Great Tit

A very familiar garden bird. Bigger than the Blue Tit and with a broad black mark down the middle of its yellow underparts.

Date....................

Place...................

Tawny Owl

Usually seen at night. Lives mainly in woodland areas. Has a large head and broad, rounded wings. Makes a familiar 'hooting' noise.

Date....................

Place...................

Barn Owl

A pale-coloured owl which looks all white in car headlights. Lives mostly in the countryside, close to farms. Makes a wild, shrieking noise.

Date.................

Place.................

Date....................

Place...................

Herring Gull

Nests on cliffs, low seashores and sometimes on the roof tops in coastal towns. Often flies inland to scavenge on rubbish dumps!

Date....................

Place...................

Puffin

Another sea-bird, mainly seen on off-shore islands or steep, inaccessible cliffs. Has a large, brightly-coloured bill.

Robin

One of our best-loved little birds. A frequent garden visitor and resident. The red breast only comes when the bird is adult.

Date....................

Place...................

Kingfisher

A small, brightly coloured bird which you will see near rivers and streams. It flies rapidly and makes a piping 'chee' sound.

Date....................

Place...................

Date....................

Place...................

Swift

Very often nests in the holes on the sides or roofs of buildings. Has long, dark wings. Makes a loud screaming noise.

Date..................

Place.................

Swallow

This bird usually lives in barns. Has a chestnut-coloured throat and long points at each side of its tail. A very graceful bird in flight.

Helping Hands

"There's a storm coming," said Badger. "I think we should find shelter quickly."

The animals had been travelling through the night, making their way from a copse where they had stopped to rest, through some fields. There were buildings in the distance, dark shadows against the early morning sky. It was just beginning to get light and a gale force wind was hurrying the thick clouds overhead and tossing the branches of the trees.

"I think you're right," agreed Fox. "What's that place up ahead?"

"Looks...like a...farm," puffed Owl, as she flew against the wind.

Although it was dry now, there had been heavy rain for several days and many of the fields were flooded.

"The river must be high," said Hedgehog. "We'll have to be very careful."

"There's a bridge," Kestrel informed them, "this side of the farm."

They hurried on, heads bent against the ever-strengthening wind.

"Quick!" Badger urged them. "I don't like the look of those trees."

And indeed, the trees at the edge of the field were swaying dangerously, groaning in the wind. By the time they reached the narrow bridge over the river, branches were beginning to

break off and drop into the water which swirled and bubbled its way downstream.

"Not far now," said Fox, pointing to the farm buildings ahead.

There were no lights on in the farmhouse... the occupants were sleeping soundly in spite of the gale. The animals could see a barn and some other outbuildings, as well as a large pig sty, its fence creaking in the wind. There seemed to be no other creatures on the farm except pigs.

"Pig farmer," guessed Fox. "Shall we try the barn?"

"Probably the best place," agreed Owl. The barn doors were warped and rotten, with several gaps in the wood large enough for even the biggest animals to crawl through. It was empty except for an ancient tractor and trailer. A newer building nearer the house, its doors and windows shut firmly, seemed the most likely place for any other machinery or stores. The old barn looked as though it was seldom used.

"Perfect," said Fox.

Badger seemed less certain. He was listening to the wind as it battered the old building.

The animals settled down in various places, and Fox found himself a corner where there was some straw on the floor. They were all tired, not because of the distance they had travelled but because it had been hard work fighting against the strong wind. Within minutes they were all fast asleep.

All except Badger, who felt suddenly thirsty. He wondered if there was a water trough for the pigs and if he could get at it. Sleep was impossible when he was thirsty.

Creeping out through one of the holes in the door, he was immediately

blown sideways by the wind. He rolled over twice before thumping against the fence around the pig sty.

"Ouch!" he grunted.

At that moment, a massive gust of wind whipped across the fields like a tornado. Badger felt the breath being knocked out of him as he was picked up again and flung against another part of the fencing round the sty. At the same time, there was a splitting sound and the fence was flattened to the ground. Suddenly, Badger was surrounded by frightened piglets, shrieking and screaming.

The shadow of a large Sow loomed over him. Fortunately, the Sow was more bothered about her offspring than a winded Badger, for the terrified piglets were running in all directions.

"Come back!" called their mother, and most of them did, gathering round the Sow and snuggling against her. But one tiny piglet kept running.

"Stop!" shouted Badger. "You're heading for the river!" And without thinking, he ran after the tiny creature.

Inside the barn, there was another calamity. The same whirlwind that had knocked down the fencing around the pig sty had sent part of the roof crashing down inside the building – right into the corner where Fox had been sleeping! Now he was trapped by great chunks of wood and corrugated tin, thankfully unhurt but quite unable to move.

"I'm stuck!" he was yelling.

"We can see that!" screamed Weasel. "We'll try and get you out!"

She and the other animals began frantically pulling off pieces of wood and tin.

"Oh dear," sobbed Mole. "Poor Fox!"

"Ssshut up and help us, you ssstupid Mole!" hissed Adder.

They managed to get most of the small pieces of wood and metal off Fox but there was one huge chunk of wooden rafter which was just too heavy for them to move.

"It's no good!" gasped Hare. "We can't shift it."

"Where's Badger?" asked Fox. "He's bigger and stronger than all of you."

And it was at that moment that everyone realised Badger was missing.

"Ooh! What are we going to do?" wailed Mole. "We've lost Badger now!"

Badger was running after the fleeing piglet as it scampered wildly this way and that. If Badger had stopped to ask himself why he was doing this, he probably would not have been able to answer. After all, Badgers cannot be responsible for the welfare of small pigs. But Badger was not without courage and he always tried to help those in need.

The piglet certainly needed help. It went skidding down the side of a slippery bank and – SPLASH! – disappeared into the water.

Badger moved more cautiously down the bank, his eyes searching the black surface of the river. And there, already being swept downstream, was the little pink head of the frightened piglet bobbing up and down in the water.

Badger looked quickly around him. His sharp eyes saw a broken tree branch and, snatching it up, he swung it towards the river.

"Grab the end of this!" he shouted to the piglet.

At first, the little animal did not seem to know what it was supposed to do, but then, as Badger swung the branch right in front of its nose, the piglet made a desperate lunge and threw itself across it, clinging tightly with its front trotters.

Badger began heaving himself back up the slippery bank, pulling the branch behind him. It took all of his strength, but after some minutes the piglet was able to scramble out of the water and up the river bank to safety.

Gasping for breath, Badger staggered back to the barn as the piglet ran past him and on towards its mother. The old Sow was waiting with her other piglets.

"Thank you!" she said to Badger. "You've saved my piglet's life!"

"Um...er...it was nothing," replied Badger, modestly. "I was glad to lend a helping hand."

The worst of the storm seemed to be over. At last the wind was beginning to drop.

"Well, I must get back to my friends," said Badger. "We've been sheltering for a while in the old barn."

"The farmer will be up soon," said

the Sow. "He'll be out to inspect the damage. You and your friends will have to make yourselves scarce."

"We'll be moving on soon," said Badger. "We've a long way to go."

Suddenly, there was a screech from the barn door behind them and Badger looked round to see Weasel.

"Badger!" screamed Weasel. "Come quickly! Fox is stuck!"

Badger ran off towards the barn. After making sure her piglets were safely bundled into a corner of the sty, the Sow followed him.

"I'm coming, too!" she called.

"Am I glad to see you!" said Fox from under the wooden rafter as Badger hurried across. "But...but who is this?"

Fox and all the other animals were staring at the Sow who was squeezing through the biggest hole in the barn door. Badger turned to look as well and smiled.

"I've brought some help," he chuckled.

"You're right," boomed the Sow. "The two of us should be able to shift that rafter."

And with one enormous HEAVE! they pushed the rafter clear of Fox.

There was a big cheer from the rest of the animals as Fox leapt free.

"Thank you," said Badger to the Sow.

"My turn to lend a helping hand," said the Sow with a smile.

A Country Walk

A game for two or more players.

It's just the day for a walk in the country – but watch out for obstacles on the way! Throw the dice and move your counter. The first person to complete the walk is the winner.

25
26
27
28
29
30
31
32
33
You wander off the proper path when crossing farmland. This could easily spoil the farmer's crops. Go back to square 25.
34
35
36
37
38
You pick up some litter that you find and put it in a rubbish bin. Have another turn.
39
40
41
Instead of using the stile, you climb over a dry-stone wall which could easily have been damaged. Miss a turn.
42
43
44
You have spotted a bluebell to enter on your flower-spotter's chart or book. Have another turn.
45
46
47
48
49
You left your empty drink can behind after your picnic. Go back to square 45.
50
End of walk.

Snakes Alive!

ANIMAL FACTS

The Adder

The adder is a small viper, and it is the only poisonous snake in Great Britain. Don't be nervous if you see one, it will probably slither away if it spots you, but do remember that it can bite so don't try to pick it up! The adder has a black band that zig-zags down its back. It feeds on frogs, mice and small mammals.

Have you seen this Flower?

On these pages are pictures of wild flowers that you can see in the British Isles. There is a space beneath each picture so that you can keep a record of the date and place you saw each flower.
Happy flower-spotting!

Lesser Celandine

Often found in damp shady woods or way-sides. It has shiny, heart-shaped leaves and yellow flowers. About 7cm tall. Seen between March and May.

Date..................

Place.................

Primrose

Very well-known wild flower. Grows in clumps and patches and can be found in woods, fields and hedgerows. About 15cm tall. Seen between February and May.

Date......................

Place.....................

Date........................

Place.......................

Ragged Robin

Has ragged pink petals and is often found in damp woods and marshes. Between 30–70cm tall. Seen in May and June.

Date..................

Place.................

Bluebell

Usually found making a beautiful blue 'carpet' in a wood or copse, in the spring. Has narrow shiny leaves. About 30cm tall. Seen between April and May.

Common Dog Violet

Pretty, low-growing plant usually found in clumps in woods and hedges. Has heart-shaped leaves. About 10–20cm tall. Can be seen flowering between April and June.

Date..................

Place................

Ox-eye Daisy

Very common flower which often grows at the sides of main roads and motorways. Up to 60cm tall. Seen between June and August.

Date.......................

Place......................

Ivy

An evergreen plant which climbs over walls and trees. Has dark shiny leaves, often with pale veins. Has black berries in the winter and white flowers between September and November.

Date....................

Place...................

Gorse

A dark green prickly bush usually found on common or heathland. Its flowers are yellow and they can be seen at all times of the year. About 1–2m tall.

Date....................

Place...................

Ragwort

Grows in all kinds of dry, grassy places. A tall plant with a flat-topped head of yellow flowers. Between 30–150cm tall. Seen flowering between June and October.

Date..................

Place.................

Honeysuckle

A climbing plant often seen in hedges and woods. Has a sweet-smelling flower, and berries which become red in the autumn. Grows up to 6m tall. Flowers between June and September.

Date................

Place...............

Mole's Free Ride

Badger was talking about the old days in Farthing Wood. He was telling Mole about all the things he could remember.

Mole was riding on Badger's back, as usual. It was early on a bright sunny morning. They could hear a tractor in a nearby field and the rattle of milk bottles on a milk float as it trundled along the country lane.

Mole was very interested in Badger's tales, but after a while they did become a *little* bit boring. Not that Mole would ever tell him that because he wouldn't want to hurt Badger's feelings.

"Sometimes," thought Mole, "I wish I had some adventures of my own to tell. But nothing particularly exciting ever happens to me."

It was when they were walking past a row of old farm cottages that Mole accidentally slipped off Badger's back and landed on the ground with a BUMP! Badger didn't even notice. He continued to tell his story even though no one was listening.

All the other animals were ahead of Badger, so they didn't see that Mole was lagging behind now, all on his own. They were trying to get to the other side of the next village before finding somewhere to settle down and rest for the day. Mole, whose eyesight wasn't very good in daylight, hadn't noticed the others were getting ahead of him. Nor did he notice something else...a large removal van with its back flap down, standing outside one of the cottages.

“Phew!” puffed Mole. “This hill is getting a bit steep. And what’s all that stuff up ahead? Looks like someone’s furniture.”

Mole reached the top of the slope and looked around.

“Hello,” he said. “I seem to have wandered into some sort of building. Or is it a room?”

But the furniture wasn’t arranged around the ‘room’, it was all piled up at the sides and at one end. Suddenly, he heard the sound of men’s voices.

“Is this the last of it, Charlie?” said one voice.

“Just this one wardrobe, yes,” said the other voice. “Then we can get moving.”

Mole looked over his shoulder and saw the two men coming towards him, carrying a large wooden thing.

“What are they doing?” he asked himself.

Thinking it might be safer not to be seen, he quickly scrambled up a heap of boxes and jumped inside the biggest one.

Luckily, Mole landed on something soft! It was dark inside the box, but he seemed to be surrounded by strange furry things. Indeed, it felt quite snug and warm in there.

Just then, he heard a BANG! like someone closing a large door. Now the whole ‘room’ became very dark.

A few moments later, there was the sound of an engine starting up and the ‘room’ began to move!

It was at this point that Mole realised he had somehow wandered into the back of a large vehicle, and that the vehicle was filled with someone’s furniture.

“Oh, no!” he groaned. “Now what am I going to do?”

The furniture van passed the other animals further along the road.

"Did you see that, Charlie?" said the driver.

"Yeah," said Charlie. "Looked like a procession of animals! Where d'you reckon they're off to? The zoo?"

"Search me," said the driver. "But you don't usually see foxes and hares walking along together, do you?"

"Maybe we should have offered them a lift!" laughed Charlie.

"Not likely!" said the driver. "We don't want any animals in the back of our van!"

The two men had started this removal job early so that they could fit in another one later. It wasn't a big job, just the belongings of a family – Mum, Dad, and two little girls – to go from the cottage out in the country to a house in the next village. It was a journey of about three miles.

"There's the house," said Charlie, as they drove through the village.

The man, his wife and their two daughters were waiting outside the front door. The man waved at the removal van to make sure Charlie and his mate had seen them. The van pulled over and stopped.

"Right," said Charlie. "Let's get this lot unloaded!"

Inside the back of the van, Mole had fallen asleep. The warm and comfortable spot he'd found in the big wooden box, and the motion of the van as it bumped along, had made him drowsy. After only a few minutes, he had been snoring. But when the van stopped, Mole woke up.

For a moment or two he couldn't think where he was, but then he remembered.

"Oh dear!" he said. "What's going to happen to me now?"

He soon found out. The back of the van was opened and in climbed the two men. They began carrying out the furniture and taking it into the house. Charlie grabbed the box Mole was in.

"Where does this go?" Charlie asked as he carried it up the garden path.

"That's our box of toys," said one of the little girls. "It goes upstairs, in our bedroom."

"Right you are, Miss," said Charlie.

He carried the big wooden tea chest into the house, up the stairs, and then dropped it on the floor of one of the bedrooms. Inside, Mole felt his stomach do a somersault as the box landed on the floor with a THUMP!

"Hooray!" shouted the little girls. "Now we can unpack our toys!"

They tipped the tea chest on its side, emptying the contents all over the floor. To his astonishment, Mole found himself rolling out of the box with some furry objects that looked remarkably like some of his friends – Badger, Fox, Rabbit, even a fluffy Owl! Except that these animals were soft, cuddly toys.

"What's that?" said one of the little girls. "I didn't know we had a mole!"

"Nor did I," said the other, as she reached out to grab Mole.

Mole quickly scuttled across the room, out of the way.

"It's a real one!" gasped one of the girls.

"Ooh, lovely!" said the other. "Perhaps Mummy will let us keep him for a pet!"

When Mole heard that, he knew he had to get out of there – and *fast*!

He made a dive for the open door and, as quickly as his little legs could carry him, he half ran, half fell down the stairs and rushed out into the garden.

"What was that?" said Charlie, seeing the little grey creature disappear into the long grass.

"It looked like another of those animals!" said his mate. "You don't think...?"

"I do think!" said Charlie. "We gave him a free ride!"

The two men began to laugh.

It was another hour before Mole's friends arrived in the village. They were very surprised to see him.

"How did you get here ahead of us?" asked Badger. "I thought you were still on my back."

"It's a long story," said Mole. "But at least now I've got an adventure I can tell *you*, for a change!"

ANIMAL FACTS

The Badger

Badgers sleep during the day and come out at night for food, so you will have to stay up late or get up very early if you want to see one! Most badgers live in the countryside and eat worms, small insects, mice, hedgehogs and plants. Sometimes they come into towns and gardens, often overturning dustbins to find food.

They have a black and white striped head, and claws to dig out their underground dens, which are called setts.

Countryside Clues

Look at the picture clues below and try to complete the crossword.

1

2

3

4

5

6

7

8

9

10

Rescue Bells

The animals were coming to the end of a long night's walk. They were all very tired. "Perhaps we could rest inside that building over there," said Badger.

"Anywhere," grumbled Weasel, "as long as I can rest my feet. I'm exhausted!" So the friends crossed the field and followed a winding path to the church.

A large wooden door was open and the animals all crept inside. "Hello?" said Vixen. "Anyone at home?" Her voice echoed around the building.

"Seems to be quiet enough," said Fox. "We're safe here." There were rows of long seats, and most of the animals settled on or underneath them.

Just then, an old man came out of a little door at the back of the building. "That's the clock wound up again," he said to himself.

He went outside and locked the door after him. He looked up at the tower to make sure the church clock was going all right, then he went home.

Inside, the animals could hear the key turning in the lock. "We shan't be able to get out!" cried Mole. "What are we going to do?"

"It might be *days* before anyone unlocks that door again," said Toad. "You've got usss into a niccce messs thisss time, Badger," grumbled Adder.

Fox went across to the little door where the old man had come from. He saw some steps. "Where do they go?" he wondered. "Could they lead us out?"

Weasel had found some ropes hanging down through the ceiling. "Perhaps if I climb up one, I'll find a way out," she thought. "It's worth a try."

Weasel pulled on one of the ropes and there was a loud DONGGGGG! She let go of it quickly. "Wh-what was that?"she said. "It's a *bell!*" said Badger.

"That gives me an idea!" he said. "We'll each pull one of the ropes and ring a bell. That should bring somebody. Come on, all of you, choose a rope!"

So the animals each took a rope and began to pull. The bells CLANGGGED and DONGGGED and made a terrible row! "What a noise!" said Toad.

"Funny time of day for bell-ringing practice," said a villager. "What's going on at the church this morning?" "There might be a wedding," said another.

But the old man knew there was no wedding that day. He hurried back to the church as fast as he could to see who was ringing the bells.

When he opened the door, the bells stopped ringing and out rushed a lot of animals! "What strange bell-ringers!" he said, chuckling to himself.

At long last, the Animals of Farthing Wood were able to begin their new lives at the Nature Reserve...

Answers to Puzzles

Pages 18 and 19: **Which Animal?**

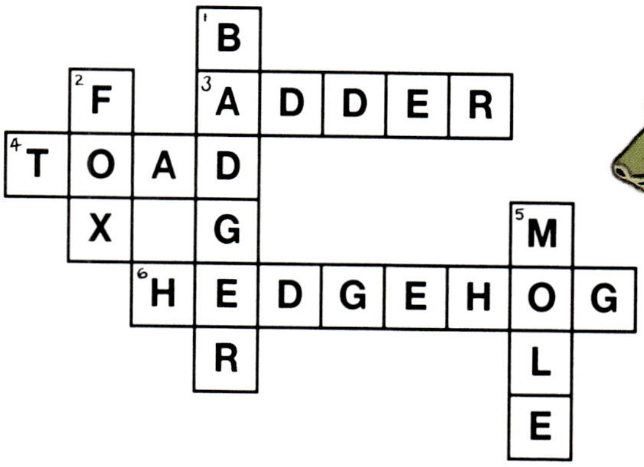

Pages 54 and 55:
Countryside Clues

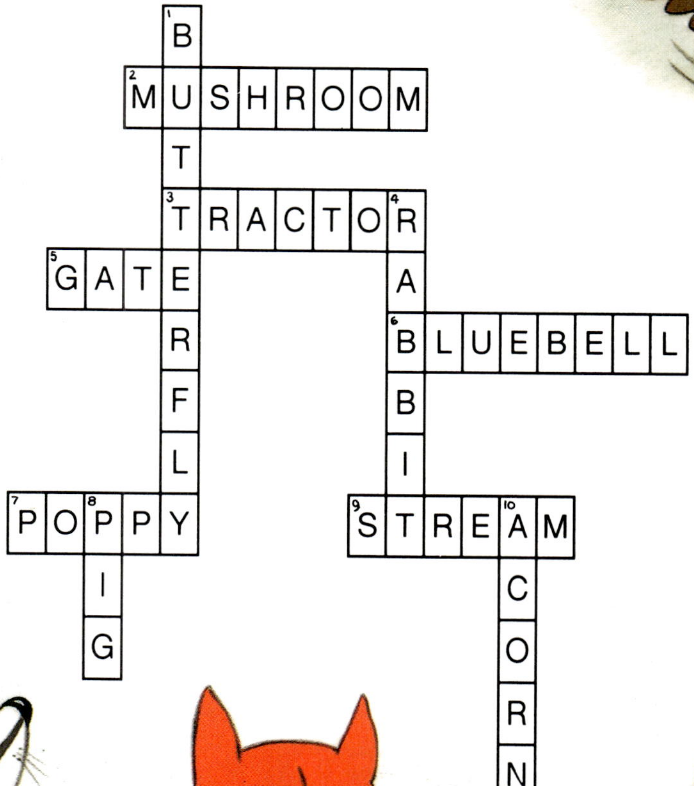

Written by John Escott.
Illustrated by Jane Swift.
Edited by Peter Nicholls.
Produced by Simon Girling & Associates,
Hadleigh, Suffolk.

Published in Great Britain in 1993 by
World International Publishing Ltd.,
an Egmont Company, Egmont House,
PO Box 111, Great Ducie Street,
Manchester M60 3BL.
Printed in Italy.
ISBN 0-7498-1355-5